# How to Become an Entrepreneurial Kid

## by Dianne Linderman

Text by
# Dianne Linderman

Edited by
Elizabeth von Radics

Layout by
Dianne Linderman and Saga Design

Library of Congress Cataloging-in-Publication Data
ISBN 0-9704876-8-1

Published by
The First Moms' Club
112 SE M Street
Grants Pass, OR 97526
www.thefirstmomsclub.com

Printed in the United States of America

# My Business Workbook

_____

# Date

_____

# Your Idea

## Everything in Life Starts with One Idea
*That's all it takes? One idea? Yes!*

When my brother Alan was 11 years old, he decided to string beads. He had very good taste for an 11-year-old boy, and he decided to get into the jewelry business. He asked my mother to take him to the local bead store to buy beads to make one necklace. He paid retail prices for his first supplies. *Retail* is the price a store sells merchandise for; when it *buys* merchandise to sell, the store pays a *wholesale* price, which is usually 50 percent less than the retail price.

*For example:* Fred's Market buys candy bars for 25 cents and sells them for 50 cents. This is a 100 percent markup. The store's profit is 25 cents per candy bar.

Your business can be selling a *product*—such as jewelry or muffins—or a *service* that you perform, such as raking leaves or cleaning houses.

# Make a List

Think up all of your ideas for a possible business and write them down here:

1. _____

2. _____

3. _____

4. _____

5. _____

6. _____

7. _____

8. _____

*Parents:* help your kids with ideas.
*Remember:* keep them simple.
Here are some examples:

Lemonade stand, kite making, bake sale, dog walking,
flower pens (pens with silk flowers, wrapped with green tape),
pet sitting, lawn mowing, yard watering, window washing, car wash,
fence painting, Internet business, make and sell crafts at craft fairs,
buy old furniture and paint and refurbish it to sell, make jewelry
to sell at school or to friends, clean and shine bikes, raise chickens
and sell eggs, sell products at an entrepreneur's marketplace,
start a publishing company and write your own books or
create a kids' newsletter and sell advertising.

# Name Your Business

A business name is very important. In a few short words,
it must describe the product or service you are selling.
Test your choices of business names on friends and family.

List your ideas for business names here:

1. _____

2. _____

3. _____

4. _____

5. _____

6. _____

7. _____

8. _____

9. _____

10. _____

# Design a Logo

## What is a logo?

A *logo* is a symbol that helps your customers identify your business. When you see the Golden Arches, you think of McDonald's; when you see the yellow star, you think of Carl's Jr. A logo can be a simple picture, or *graphic*, of something that has to do with what you are selling. If you have a dog-walking business, for example, draw a picture of a dog and put the name of your business with it. Keep the logo simple; all it really *must* have is your business name.

Here are two examples of simple logos. Look for logos on TV, in magazines, in newspapers, and on packaging for inspiration. Then start by sketching out ideas of logos for your business. You can do this on pages 18 and 19.

# Start-up Costs
## Make a list of everything you'll need to start your business.

Once you have your idea, your business name, and a logo, the next step is to figure out your start-up costs. Begin by making a list of *product costs* (what it costs you to purchase the item for sale) or *equipment costs* (what it costs you to purchase the equipment for performing your service). *Start-up costs* include your tape, paper, marking pens, calculator, or whatever you need to get started. This also includes the cost of photocopying your flyer or brochure (see "Market Your Business" on pages 12 and 13.)

1. _____ Cost $_____
2. _____ Cost $_____
3. _____ Cost $_____
4. _____ Cost $_____
5. _____ Cost $_____
6. _____ Cost $_____
7. _____ Cost $_____
8. _____ Cost $_____
9. _____ Cost $_____
10. _____ Cost $_____

Total $_____

# Material Costs.
## Make a list of raw materials

If you will be selling a product, make a complete list of the *raw materials* you will need or the wholesale prices you will pay. If you are going to make beaded jewelry, for example, the raw materials are the beads and the string; if you will be selling lemonade, you will first need to buy lemons, sugar, and paper cups.

1. _____ Cost $_____
2. _____ Cost $_____
3. _____ Cost $_____
4. _____ Cost $_____
5. _____ Cost $_____
6. _____ Cost $_____
7. _____ Cost $_____
8. _____ Cost $_____
9. _____ Cost $_____
10. _____ Cost $_____

Total $_____

# Finance Your Business
## Earn the money to launch your venture.

Once you know what you want to sell and how much it will cost to get started, you need to figure out how to raise the money for your start-up costs. I believe that all kids should learn how to make their own start-up money. If parents see that their kids are actually working hard, however, they can help out. When children work hard for their start-up money, they will be more committed to their business, and it won't end up being a passing phase. There are hundreds of ways to make start-up money. Here are just a few ideas:

Doing house chores      Mowing lawns

Walking dogs      Washing cars or boats

Picking fruit      Babysitting

Washing windows      Pulling weeds

Delivering groceries      Making and selling crafts

Raking leaves      Doing errands

Having a garage sale      Delivering newspapers

Pet sitting      Being a "mother's helper"

Take out trash
Wash dishes
Clean cellar
Mow lawn
Wash car

# Make a List

Think up all of your ideas for ways to earn
the start-up money for your business.

1. _____

2. _____

3. _____

4. _____

5. _____

6. _____

7. _____

8. _____

9. _____

10. _____

# Market Your Business

Once you have your idea, business name, logo, and start-up money, you need to start *marketing* your product or service. This means how and to whom you sell it. Marketing also needs a plan: First you decide who will be buying your product or service—this is your *target market*. Will you be selling cookies to local kids? Doing yard work for neighborhood adults? Going to craft fairs or flea markets and selling items to the general public? Targeting people on the Internet? Having a garage sale? Wherever you decide to sell your product or service, you need to *advertise*. Start by making a flyer or brochure. Here's what it should include:

Your business name

Your logo

Your name

Your phone number

Your address (*optional*—get your parents approval for this)

A brief description of what you are selling

The cost of the product or service

A picture or graphic related to your product or service

# Market Your Business *(continued)*

The flyer or brochure should be professional and easy to understand. It should be clear to the customer what you are offering and how much it costs. You can make your advertisement by hand or with a computer, but be sure that it's neat and that you spell everything correctly.

The next step in marketing your product or service is passing out your flyer or brochure. You can put it in people's mailboxes, hang it on public bulletin boards, or leave it on car windshields. If you have a product to sell, you can go to craft fairs, flea markets, and garage sales. My son sells his products at our own garage sales and has made as much as $110 in one day.

There are many other places to set up your concession. When you start to make a little money, you can advertise in local newspapers. You can also create a Web site to promote your product or service on the Internet.

# Bookkeeping

It is very important to keep track of your finances—how much you are spending to run your business (expenses) and how much money you are making (income). You will also need to know what your profit is; profit is the amount of money that is left over after you pay your start-up costs and expenses. On pages 16 and 17 is a simple worksheet for you. Once your business is under way, you can "keep your books" in a ledger or notebook.

# Bank Account

Once you have made some money, you need to start a savings account at a bank. This is a very good way to keep track of your income. You can also collect interest on your savings—a percentage of your money that the bank pays you. The more you deposit in the bank, the more interest you make. Many banks have programs designed to help kids understand finances. Check with the local banks to see what kinds of programs they have for kids.

# Legal Stuff

Now that you understand how to start a business, you have one more very important area to take care of—the legal stuff!

When you start a business, one of the most important things to do is to call your local city offices to find out where you can apply for a business license. Ask what else you need to do to start your own business. Find the right people and ask a lot of questions.

Write down your answers:

_____

_____

_____

Research the local regulations on the type of business you are thinking of starting. If you are offering a service, find out if you would need a license. If you are considering being a handyman, for example, you might need a contractor's license. Make a list below and start making your phone calls:

_____

_____

_____

# Bookkeeping Worksheet

## Start-up Costs

*Sample:*

Pencils
Pens
Calculator

1. _____
2. _____
3. _____
4. _____
5. _____
6. _____
7. _____
8. _____
9. _____
10. _____
11. _____
12. _____
Total _____

## Start-up Costs

*Sample:*

Wood
Glue
Paper

1. _____
2. _____
3. _____
4. _____
5. _____
6. _____
7. _____
8. _____
9. _____
10. _____
11. _____
12. _____
Total _____

# Bookkeeping Worksheet (continued)

## Expenses

*Sample:*

Phone
Pay for help
Space rent

1. _____
2. _____
3. _____
4. _____
5. _____
6. _____
7. _____
8. _____
9. _____
10. _____
11. _____
12. _____

Total _____

**Total expenses:** _____

**Total cost of goods:** _____

*Figure only what you used to make the products sold.*

**Total income:** _____

*This is how much you actually made.*

**Grand total:** _____

**Profit:** _____

*If you have extra materials, consider those as a part of your profit.*

# Notes, Ideas, and Sketches

# Notes, Ideas, and Sketches

# Now Go for It!

The best thing about having your own business is that you'll keep getting new ideas—ways that you can add to your business or change it for the better. Don't worry if you don't make a profit the first time. You have to keep working at your business to make a success of it.

If your venture is not making a lot of money, you can always come up with different ways of marketing it. This is *your* business, but don't be afraid to get ideas from other people, especially your parents. Remember that you are in control of your own future, and giving up is no way to succeed. If it's not working out, change it! Grownups do it in their businesses every day. Life is about trying new things until they work.

It's like building a model airplane: If you buy a model off the store shelf, it will end up a beautiful airplane that someone else designed. But if you get a piece of wood and whittle it to *your* design, it may not be the most beautiful design, but it is yours; and if you keep practicing, it will get better. One day you might want to design a *real* airplane! Most of the successful entrepreneurs in the world started with one simple idea, *and they did not give up.*

It's all about having an adventure, working for something you believe in, and having fun. Even if your plans don't work the first time, the fun is in trying and following through with a venture of your own.

Good luck—and keep in touch! I would love to hear from you. You can write to me at ***dianne@thefirstmomsclub.com***.